SARAH, PLAIN AND TALL

by
Patricia MacLachlan

Teacher Guide

Written by
Phyllis A. Green

Note

The Harper Trophy paperback edition of the book was used to prepare this guide. The page references may differ in other editions.

Please note: Please assess the appropriateness of this book for the age level and maturity of your students prior to reading and discussing it with your class.

ISBN 1-56137-247-1

To order, contact your local school supply store, or—

Novel Units, Inc.
P.O. Box 791610
San Antonio, TX 78279

Web site: www.educyberstor.com

Table of Contents

Skills and Strategies

Thinking
   Brainstorming, comparing
   and contrasting, evaluating,
   analyzing details

Literary Elements
   Character, setting, plot
   development, figurative
   language

Vocabulary
   Compound words, prefixes/
   suffixes, synonyms

Comprehension
   Predicting, sequencing,
   cause/effect, inference

Writing
   Narrative, descriptive

Listening/Speaking
   Participation in discussion
   and cooperative groups,
   entertain others with
   dramatic activities

Summary of *Sarah, Plain and Tall*

Sarah, Plain and Tall, a Newbery Award winner, details the courtship of a mail-order bride. Sarah responds to a newspaper advertisement placed by a plains farmer with two young children. The efforts by the children and Papa to make the prairie appealing to a plain and tall Sarah from a Maine seacoast town are delightful. The story is written for 8- to 10-year-olds in a simple style, developing the growing personal relationships and revealing quite a bit about late-19th-century prairie life.

About the Newbery Award

The medal is named for eighteenth-century British bookseller John Newbery. It is awarded annually by the Association for Library Service to Children, a division of the American Library Association, to the author of the most distinguished contribution to American literature for children.

About the Author

Patricia MacLachlan graduated from the University of Connecticut. She was born in Cheyenne, Wyoming and lives in western Massachusetts with her husband and three children. She says that the idea for *Sarah, Plain and Tall* came from a family incident. Other books by Patricia MacLachlan include *Arthur, For the Very First Time, Cassie Binegar, Unclaimed Treasures.*

Initiating Activities

1. "Did Mama sing every day?" asked Caleb—the first sentence of the book—gives us some clues about *Sarah, Plain and Tall.* Put on your detective hat and try to answer the following who, what, where, when, and why questions.

Who is Caleb?	*(boy)*
What is his situation?	*(doesn't know his mother)*
Where does he live?	*(not sure)*
When did he ask the question?	*(at dusk)*
Is Caleb a common name?	*(no, not very popular)*
When was it popular?	*(late nineteenth century)*

   Why would he ask the question? *(His mother is not available to answer herself. She is dead.)*

2. Why would a book receive the Newbery Medal? What do you expect from it because of the award? Have you read any other Newbery winners? Did you like those books? Why?

3. Make a bookmark to use while reading this book. List three predictions you have for the book on it. (The bookmark is suitable for duplication for each student.)

■ *Sarah, Plain and Tall* ■

✍ *My first prediction:*

✍ *My second prediction:*

✍ *My third prediction:*

■ *Sarah, Plain and Tall* ■

✍ *My first prediction:*

✍ *My second prediction:*

✍ *My third prediction:*

■ *Sarah, Plain and Tall* ■

✍ *My first prediction:*

✍ *My second prediction:*

✍ *My third prediction:*

Chapter 1, pp. 3-10

Vocabulary

hearthstones 3	troublesome 4	homely 5	holler 5
horrid 5	wretched 5	prairie 5	advertisement 8
shuffling 8	energetic 9	opinions 9	

Discussion Questions

1. Why didn't Papa sing anymore? *(His wife had died when his younger child was born.)*

2. What does Anna think is the worst thing about Caleb? *(Mama died the next morning after Caleb was born.)*

3. What is the setting of this story? When and where did it occur? *(late-nineteenth-century prairie)* Support your answer with evidence from the book.

4. Explain why "tears came" to Anna on page 6. *(She remembered her mother and was sorry for Caleb who didn't remember her.)*

5. What does Mr. Witting think might be a way to remember the old songs? *(to find a mail-order bride and mother for Caleb and Anna)*

6. Who is telling the story? *(Anna)*

Supplementary Activities

1. Attribute Web: Start attribute webs for each of the characters in the book. (See activity sheets on pages 28-31.)

2. Writing: Write a set of questions which others reading the book should be able to answer. Then exchange your questions with another student who will find answers.

3. Writing: If you were going to write a story about your family or your grandparents or great grandparents who lived during the early 1900s, how would you start the story? Discuss the ways stories start and then write a first paragraph for your own family saga (story).

Chapter 2, pp. 11-15

Vocabulary

fogbound 11   flounder 11   pesky 12   shingles 13
pitchfork 14

Discussion Questions

1. **Prediction:** What are the first questions you would ask a prospective mother?

2. Where does Sarah live? *(Maine)* What do we learn about Sarah's home from her letters? *(She lives near the ocean, with a lot of fish and sea birds living nearby.)*

3. How do Anna and Caleb feel about Sarah? *(They are excited and anxious about meeting her and making a good impression.)* Support your answer with evidence from the book.

4. Who is Seal? *(Sarah's cat)* Describe her (p. 13).

5. What did Sarah write at the end of her letters to Jacob? *(a message to Anna and Caleb that she sings)*

6. Complete the analysis page on the following page to summarize what you know so far and predict how she will react to Anna, Caleb, and Jacob.

Supplementary Activities

1. Writing: Does this book remind you of any other books you've read? Explain your answer in three or four sentences.

2. Writing: Describe a pet of yours. First review how Sarah describes Seal.

3. Art: Draw a picture of Seal.

4. Analysis: Begin to fill in a story map to summarize and analyze the story.

Investigation and Analysis of Sarah

1. What information do you have about Sarah so far? Include descriptions and adjectives.

2. What problems might develop when Sarah visits Caleb, Anna, and Jacob?

3. What hopeful signs do you see in the book for Sarah to like Anna, Caleb, and Jacob?

Investigation and Analysis of Sarah

1. What information do you have about Sarah so far? Include descriptions and adjectives.

   - from Maine

   - lives by the sea

   - strong

   - works hard

   - not mild mannered

   - willing to travel

   - favorite colors are blue, gray, and green

2. What problems might develop when Sarah visits Caleb, Anna, and Jacob?

   - Sarah might be disillusioned by the prairie and the isolation of Jacob's home.

   - Sarah may lack knowledge to function in Jacob's home.

3. What hopeful signs do you see in the book for Sarah to like Anna, Caleb, and Jacob?

   - Sarah sings.

   - Sarah seems to like children.

   - Anna, Caleb, and Jacob are anxious to please Sarah.

Chapter 3, pp. 16-21

Vocabulary

Indian paintbrush 16	wild-eyed 16	marsh hawk 18
windbreak 18	flax 21	

Discussion Questions

1. **Prediction:** "Sarah came in the spring" is the first sentence in Chapter 3. What do you think Sarah will see in a prairie spring?

2. How can you tell that the day in Chapter 3 is a special day? *(Papa brushes his hair slick and shiny, wears a clean blue shirt and a belt instead of suspenders. Caleb and Anna do their chores quietly and then wait nervously. Anna rocks on the porch and Caleb rolls a marble back and forth. Sarah wears a yellow bonnet.)*

3. What did Sarah bring to show Caleb and Anna the sea? *(a moon snail shell for Caleb and a sea stone for Anna)*

4. What was the look that Anna noticed and concerned her? *(loneliness on Sarah's face)*

5. What is loneliness? *(Answers vary.)* Share incidences of loneliness you've experienced. Make a list of adjectives to describe loneliness. How have you conquered loneliness? How do you think Sarah will get over her loneliness? What might Anna, Caleb, and Jacob do to help?

6. How old is Anna? *(Answers vary.)* Support your answers with evidence from the book.

7. Where do you think Seal will live? Why? *(Answers vary.)*

Supplementary Activities

1. Writing: Write a short paragraph to explain what you've learned in the book.

2. Biology: Investigate some of the plants and animals mentioned in the book. (See page 20.)

3. Interview: Interview someone who has lived by the sea.

Chapter 4, pp. 22-27

Vocabulary

| scallop 22 | paddock 23 | bride's bonnet 23 | goldenrod 24 |
| asters 24 | woolly ragwort 24 | | |

Discussion Questions

1. **Prediction:** Who do you think will love Sarah first?

2. What was Sarah's prized collection? *(shells to remind her of the sea and Maine)*

3. Caleb so wants Sarah to stay that he notices any clue or sign. List some of his childish logic that Sarah will stay. *(Sarah is drying flowers for winter. Sarah spoke of looking for nests of curls later.)*

4. What does "ayuh" mean? *(yes)* Try using the term for a whole day.

5. What singing is there in Chapter 4? *(Caleb made up a woolly ragwort song. Sarah taught the family "Summer is Icumen In." A meadowlark sang at the end of the chapter.)*

6. Look back over the whole book, reviewing references to singing. Why does an author use a continuing theme, like singing, in a book? *(to provide a thread of continuity holding the book together, to allow for development and change)*

Chapter 5, pp. 28-32

Vocabulary

| buzzards 28 | dune 29 | mica 29 |

Discussion Questions

1. **Prediction:** Why would Sarah begin to smile?

2. What does Jacob find as a dune? *(hay mound)*

3. Why is it important to Caleb that Sarah calls the hay mound "our dune"? *(It's an indication that Sarah is thinking of the prairie as her home.)*

4. If you were trying to recreate a dune in your area, what would you use? Explain why.

Supplementary Activities

1. Make some charcoal drawings of the prairie as Sarah has done. Choose *one* color of charcoal or crayon for your work. Explain your choice of color.

2. Write a vivid description of an interesting character in the story. Why would the character make a nice addition to your family? Or why not? (Characters could be people or pets.)

3. Dramatize the chapter. Choose narrators to read the chapter aloud while the rest of the class acts out the parts.

Chapter 6, pp. 33-37

Vocabulary

reins 33   gullies 35   treaded 37

Discussion Questions

1. **Prediction:** "The days grew longer." When are the days longer? What are the activities when days are longer?

2. How do Caleb and Anna describe winter? *(cold, go to school, lots of snow, ice on the windows, warm fire in fireplace, windy)*

3. How do those in Maine and on the prairie solve caring for animals in winter? *(In Maine, sometimes barns are attached to houses. On the prairie, farmers tie a rope from the house to the barn so no one will get lost when looking after the animals.)*

4. What happens in the cow pond? *(Sarah takes Caleb and Anna swimming.)*

5. How do you think swimming in the ocean is different from swimming in the cow pond? *(The ocean is salty, large, and the waves are large. The cow pond is much smaller and is fresh water.)*

Supplementary Activities

1. Customs: How do your friends or family members find someone to marry? Why does Papa use a different method?

2. Letter Writing: Write a letter from Sarah to her brother in Maine describing her adventures through Chapter 6.

Chapter 7, pp. 38-43

Vocabulary

whickering 38	zinnias 41	marigolds 41	feverfew 41
dahlias 41	columbine 41	nasturtiums 41	tansy 42

Discussion Questions

1. **Prediction:** Notice how the chapters start. When do you think this chapter will take place?

2. Who are Matthew and Maggie? *(neighbors)* Have you met them earlier in the book? *(No, but there is a reference to Matthew and his mail-order bride, Maggie, on page 8.)* Why? *(They must live some distance away and not be able to visit often.)*

3. Why did Sarah's eyes fill with tears? *(She misses her brother and aunts in Maine. She is reminded of the feeling when Maggie visits and recognizes Sarah's loneliness.)*

4. Was Anna right about the chickens? *(yes)* How did she know she was right? *(Sarah wanted to name the chickens, making them pets. It would be hard to eat a pet.)*

5. What is special about Sarah's garden? *(She is putting down roots and will try to grow some Maine flowers.)*

6. How does Papa show he likes Sarah? *(He brought her the first roses of the summer.)*

Chapter 8, pp. 44-50

Vocabulary

sly 45	squall 47	pungent 47	milled 48

Discussion Questions

1. **Prediction:** Why has Caleb been worried throughout the book? What signs has he seen? What are some other signs he might see? (You can look back at Chapters 1-7 to remind yourself.)

2. Why do you think Sarah wants to learn how to ride Jack? *(Answers vary, but may include the idea that Maggie inspired her to gain some independence by going into town by herself.)*

3. What is Caleb's reaction to Sarah's request to learn to ride? *(alarm; He is afraid Sarah may go into town by herself and leave the family.)*

4. What does the family do to prepare for the storm? Fill in your answers on the left side of a T-chart. Then fill in the right side of the T-chart to detail how you would prepare for a summer storm.

How Sarah, Jacob, Caleb and Anna prepare for storm	How I would prepare for storm
• fix the roof	
• collect the animals in the barn	
• assemble the family in the barn during the storm	

5. What did they see after the storm? *(hail on the ground; "Like sun on glass. Like the sea.")*

6. How would you describe hail? *(Answers vary.)* The author used a simile to describe the hail on page 50. What is a simile? *(A comparison using "like" or "as.")*

Chapter 9, pp. 51-58

Vocabulary
scuttling 52

Discussion Questions
1. **Prediction:** How will the story end? Support your answer with clues from the book.

2. What are some of Caleb's suggestions to keep Sarah with them? *(get sick, tie her up)*

3. Why did Sarah kiss them all when she went on her first solo wagon trip to town? *(Answers vary, but may include ideas that she cares for them. Kissing is also an appropriate good-bye gesture.)*

4. Anna makes a comparison between Sarah going to town in the wagon and the wagon that took her mother away. Find that recollection and read it aloud (p. 54). Fill in the Venn diagram about the two wagon trips.

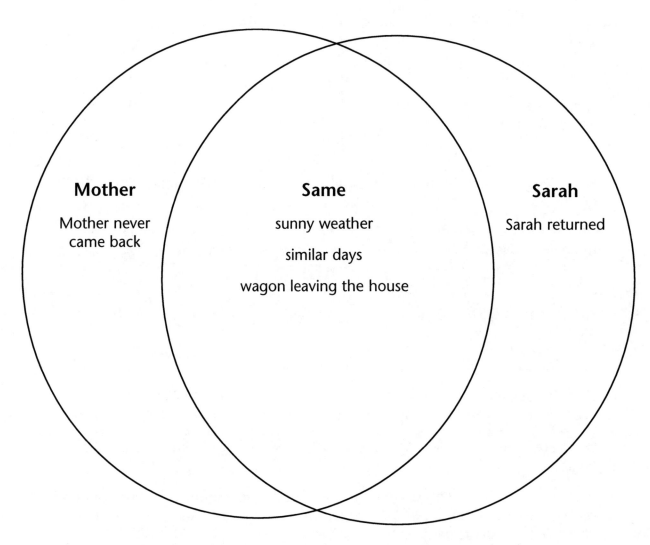

Mother

Mother never came back

Same

sunny weather

similar days

wagon leaving the house

Sarah

Sarah returned

How do Venn diagrams vary as to the positioning of the two circles? *(The greater the amount of similarity, the greater part of the circles will overlap.)*

5. Why does Sarah go to town? *(The immediate errand is to buy a special present for Caleb and Anna. A deeper reason might be for Sarah to feel personally independent and to share the sea colors with Caleb and Anna.)*

6. Why do you think the author used italics for the last two paragraphs? *(Answers vary, but may include the idea that the final two paragraphs should be emphasized, that they resolve the story.)*

Post-reading Activities

1. Discuss what the author's message in the book is.

2. Play the spinner game which summarize the book's ideas. (See page 21.)

3. Review the nine chapters of the book and suggest chapter titles that could be used.

4. Think of a different ending for the story. Write it up in a short paragraph. Write a letter to the author to explain your new ending.

5. Obtain a video of the made-for-television production of *Sarah, Plain and Tall*. View it. How is the television drama different from the book? How is it similar to the book?

Supplementary Activities

1. Diagramming: The main characters are Sarah, Caleb, Anna, and Jacob. Plot their feelings as the story progresses. (See Emotions Chart on page 23.)

2. Comparison: Make a bulletin board comparison of Maine and the prairie, using a map of the United States as the background.

3. Venn Diagram: Use a Venn diagram to compare seacoast and prairie. (See page 32.)

4. Writing: Have students write paragraphs describing characters without naming the person. Read the descriptions and let everyone guess who is being described.

5. Writing: Write the next chapter to the book.

6. Writing: Write an advertisement to be placed in a newspaper across the country for a new family member—a pet.

7. Writing: Write a letter to William dated a year after Sarah and Jacob are married.

8. Writing: Make a change in the story and tell why in a short paragraph.

© Novel Units, Inc.

15

9. Drama: If you were directing the television movie, "Sarah, Plain and Tall," who would you cast as actors and actresses?

10. Classifying: Plants and animals are mentioned extensively in the book. A listing is included on page 20. You can laminate and use for sorting into prairie and seacoast stacks. Students can prepare a class book with pictures/drawings of each of the plants and animals.

11. Etymology: The names are interesting in this book. Keep a list of the characters, looking up the origin and meaning of the names. What do the names have in common? Have you heard them frequently?

Caleb	Jacob	Sarah	Maggie
Lottie	Nick	Jack	Matthew
Anna	William	Rose	Violet

12. Social Studies: Read the novel as part of a social studies unit on prairies or Illinois or any prairie state.

13. Science: Use the novel in conjunction with plant or animal unit.

14. Science: The book describes the four seasons. Make webs for each season.

15. Mathematics: Discuss how the family in the story used mathematics in their daily lives.

16. Mathematics: Have students write story problems to be exchanged with classmates using the characters and events in the story.

17. Similes: Look for similes (comparisons using "like" or "as") in the book. Then translate the simile either in a short sentence or by drawing a picture.

Vocabulary Words

hearthstones	troublesome	homely	holler	horrid
wretched	prairie	advertisement	shuffling	energetic
opinions	fogbound	flounder	pesky	shingles
pitchfork	Indian paintbrush	flax	wild-eyed	marsh hawk
windbreak	scallop	paddock	bride's bonnet	goldenrod
asters	woolly ragwort	tansy	whickering	zinnias
marigolds	feverfew	dahlias	columbine	nasturtiums
sly	squall	pungent	milled	scuttling

Vocabulary Activities

1. Play "Dictionary" with meanings of the words. Or play Pictionary with pictures drawn to identify the words. Students compile their own individual dictionaries. The teachers may assemble blank booklets to be filled in.

2. Play Bingo. (Use sheets included suitable for laminating or duplicating for all students.) Prompt is the definition of the word. Students can use a blank grid, filling in vocabulary words wherever they choose. The game can also be played with definitions written on the grids and words as the prompts.

3. Student chooses (or is given) a word to compose an advertisement to "sell" his or her word.

4. Student sorts the vocabulary words according to part of speech (describers, names, actions).

5. Be a detective. Teacher writes a definition on the board. Students match the definitions with their individual vocabulary words.

6. Write words the way they feel. For example:

   tiny   or   l o n g

7. Draw a face to describe the emotion of your vocabulary word.

8. Play hangman with the words (or definitions) either with teams, the entire class, or in pairs.

9. Choose a word or words of the day to focus on. Highlight the word in the morning exercises and have everyone look for the word or words throughout the day.

10. Start class synonym chains on which students keep adding synonyms for a given prompt word. For example: *move*—run—walk—hobble—skip—drive.

11. Have students prepare crossword puzzles using vocabulary words. Trade with other students to solve the puzzles.

12. Use the vocabulary sheets cut apart into flash cards so pairs of students can "test" each other.

Teacher Background on Prairies

Definition
Prairies are areas of level or nearly level land covered chiefly by tall grasses which often grow as tall as a man when left uncultivated.

American History
American pioneers who first saw the Midwest flat prairies described them as a "sea of grass." The American prairie has largely disappeared. Fields of corn and wheat now cover most of the area.

Geography
The North American prairie region extends from central Texas to southern Saskatchewan. East to west it extends from central Illinois to the foothills of the Rocky Mountains. Most of Oklahoma, Kansas, Nebraska, Iowa, Illinois, South Dakota, and North Dakota as well as parts of nearby states are included in the North American prairie. Canadian provinces of Alberta, Saskatchewan, and Manitoba are called the prairie provinces. Prairies occur in every continent except Antarctica: the Pampa of Argentina, the veld of South Africa, and parts of Hungary, Romania, and central Russia.

Climate and Soil
Prairies have hot summers, cold winters, and moderate rainfall. The soil is especially deep, with dark, fertile upper layers. At the end of the growing season, the heavy grass cover dies away, returning nutrients to the soil. The deep roots of the grasses form a fibrous mass of vegetable matter that adds humus to the soil.

Vegetation
In addition to the tall grasses, there are a variety of flowers such as asters, blazing stars, coneflowers, goldenrods, sunflowers, clovers, psoraleas, wild indigos, phlox, butterfly weed, shooting stars, and prairie lilies.

Animals
A variety of animals proliferate on the prairie, including prairie dogs, jack rabbits, coyotes, foxes, skunks, hawks, owls, elk, badgers, gophers, and quail. Until the late 1800s, large herds of bison roamed the American prairie.

Plants and Animals Mentioned in *Sarah, Plain and Tall*

flounder	sea bass	bluefish	seal	lambs
Russian Olive	woodchuck	blue-eyed grass	sheep	cows
turtles	gulls	moon snail	dogs	sea clam
oyster	Indian paintbrush	cat	razor clam	marsh hawk
conch	scallop	clover	bride's bonnet	goldenrod
asters	woolly ragwort	tansy	spruce	zinnias
marigolds	feverfew	dahlias	columbine	nasturtiums
pine	spruce	killdeer	banty chickens	dandelions
horses	corn	wild roses	prairie violets	meadowlark
buzzards	whales	crows	wild daisies	prairie grass

© Novel Units, Inc.

Spinner Game

Directions: Use the circle with a spinner. Each student (or small group) takes a turn to spin and to answer.

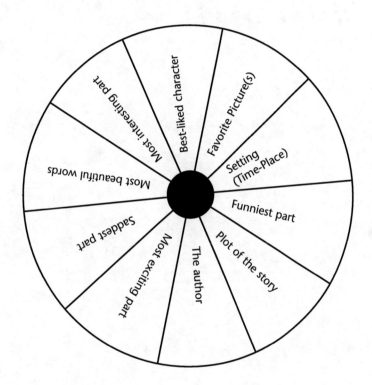

Bulletin Board Ideas

1. Students make up their own "people" to include on the board, using their own name and two adjectives.

What's In a Name?

Sarah

plain,

tall

2. Divide bulletin board into sections for seacoast and prairie, using blue as a back ground for the seacoast and beige for the prairie. Have students decorate the sections using quotations and ideas from the book as well as ideas from their research on the plants mentioned in the book.

3. Divide the bulletin board into sections to display reports on the plants and animals mentioned in the book. (See list on page 20.)

Emotions Chart

Directions: For each of the characters listed, provide a sketch and a phrase describing his or her emotions in each chapter. For example, in Chapter 1, Caleb might be described as curious about his mother.

	1	2	3	4	5	6	7	8	9
Chapters									
Characters									
Caleb									
Anna									
Jacob									
Sarah									

Follow-up activity: In a short paragraph, summarize how one of the characters developed and changed emotionally through the book.

Bio-Poem

Directions: Write a Bio-poem for one of the characters in the book.

—A pattern poem

—Line 1:   First name only

—Line 2:   Four traits that describe that person

—Line 3:   Sibling of …(or son/daughter of…)

—Line 4:   Lover of …(three people or ideas)

—Line 5:   Who feels…(three items)

—Line 6:   Who fears…(three items)

—Line 7:   Who would like to see…(three items)

—Line 8:   Resident of…(city, state, street, etc.)

—Line 9:   Last name only

—May extend to 11 lines. Between lines 6 and 7 add:

    —Who needs…(three items)

    —Who gives…(three items)

1 _____

2 _____

3 _____

4 _____

5 _____

6 _____

7 _____

8 _____

9 _____

10 _____

11 _____

Using Predictions

We all make predictions as we read—little guesses about what will happen next, how the conflict will be resolved, which details given by the author will be important to the plot, which details will help to fill in our sense of a character. Students should be encouraged to predict, to make sensible guesses. As students work on predictions, these discussion questions can be used to guide them: What are some of the ways to predict? What is the process of a sophisticated reader's thinking and predicting? What clues does an author give us to help us in making our predictions? Why are some predictions more likely than others?

A predicting chart is for students to record their predictions. As each subsequent chapter is discussed, you can review and correct previous predictions. This procedure serves to focus on predictions and to review the stories.

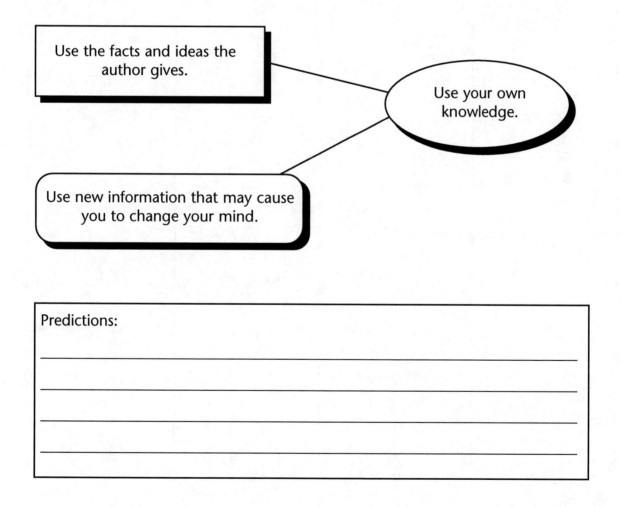

Predictions:

_____

_____

_____

_____

Prediction Chart

What characters have we met so far?	What is the conflict in the story?	What are your predictions?	Why did you make those predictions?

Story Map

Characters_____

_____

```
┌──────────┐
│ Setting  │
└──────────┘
     │
     ▼
```

Time and Place_____

_____

```
┌──────────┐
│ Problem  │
└──────────┘
     │
     ▼
```

Problem_____

_____

_____

```
┌──────────┐
│  Goal    │
└──────────┘
     │
     ▼
```

Goal_____

_____

_____

Beginning ⟶ Development ⟶ Outcome

```
┌──────────┐
│ Episodes │
└──────────┘
     │
     ▼
```

_____

_____

_____

_____

```
┌────────────┐
│ Resolution │
└────────────┘
```

Resolution_____

_____

_____

_____

Using Character Webs

Attribute Webs are simply a visual representation of a character from the novel. They provide a systematic way for the students to organize and recap the information they have about a particular character. Attribute webs may be used after reading the novel to recapitulate information about a particular character or completed gradually as information unfolds, done individually, or finished as a group project.

One type of character attribute web uses these divisions:

• How a character acts and feels. (How does the character feel in this picture? How would you feel if this happened to you? How do you think the character feels?)

• How a character looks. (Close your eyes and picture the character. Describe him to me.)

• Where a character lives. (Where and when does the character live?)

• How others feel about the character. (How does another specific character feel about our character?)

In group discussion about the student attribute webs and specific characters, the teacher can ask for backup proof from the novel. You can also include inferential thinking.

Attribute webs need not be confined to characters. They may also be used to organize information about a concept, object or place.

Attribute Web

The attribute web below will help you gather clues the author provides about a character in the novel. Fill in the blanks with words and phrases which tell how the character acts and looks, as well as what the character says and what others say about him or her.

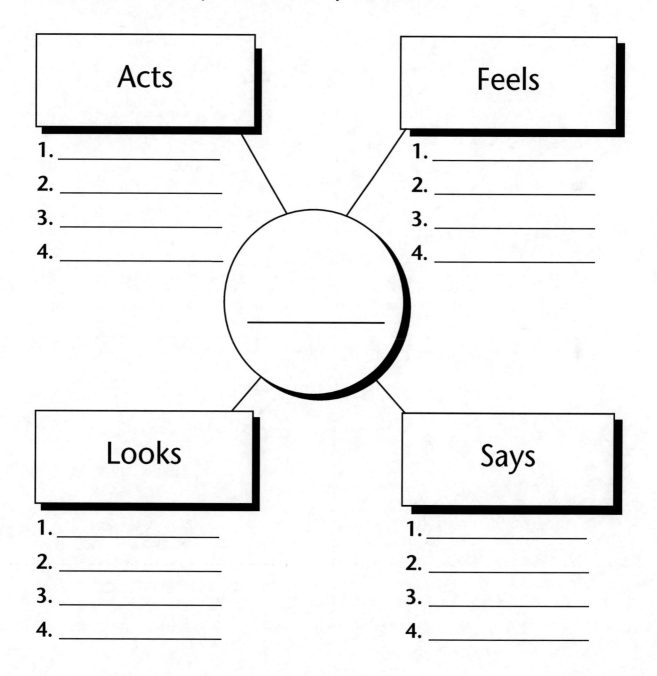

Acts

1. _____
2. _____
3. _____
4. _____

Feels

1. _____
2. _____
3. _____
4. _____

Looks

1. _____
2. _____
3. _____
4. _____

Says

1. _____
2. _____
3. _____
4. _____

Attribute Web

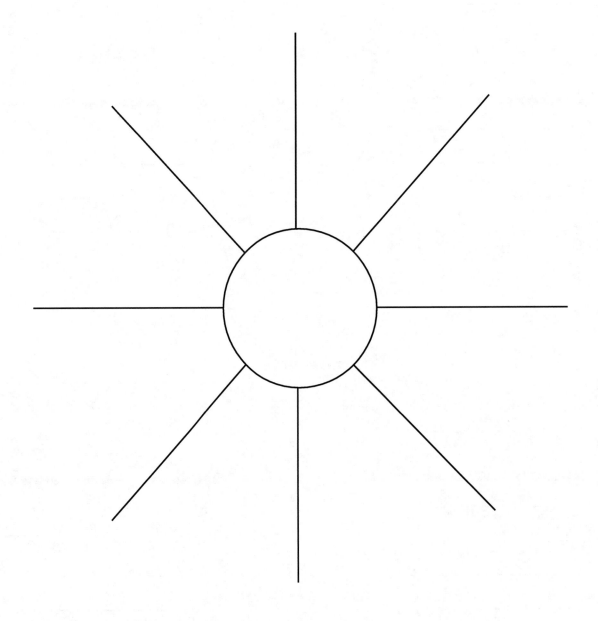

Completed Attribute Webs

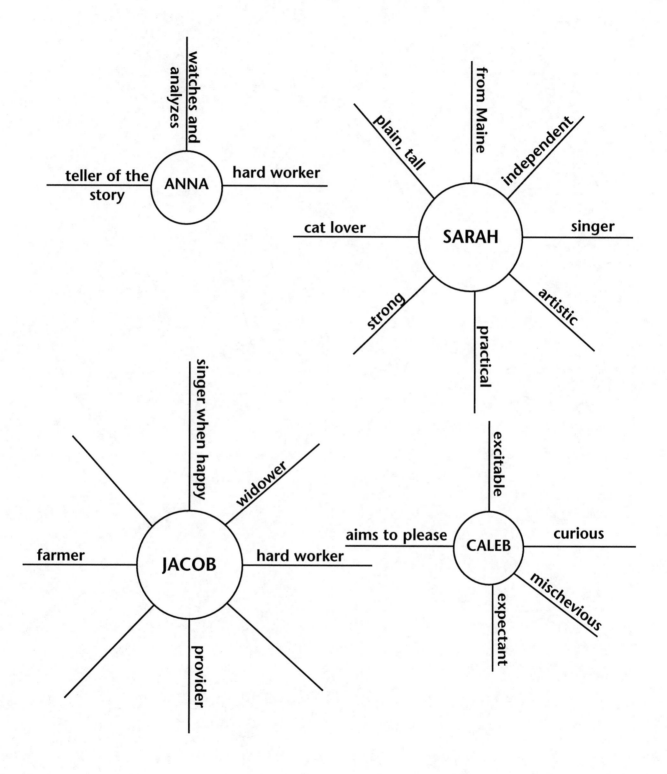

Venn Diagram

Prairie   **Seacoast**

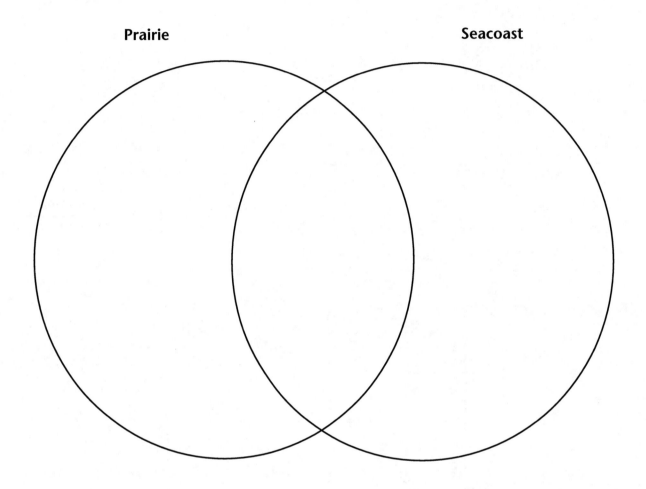

Novel Units® Teacher Guides and Student Packets

NU6105	NU6113SP	Watsons Go To Birmingham
NU4806		Weasel
NU5950		When Hitler Stole Pink Rabbit
NU7376		Which Way Freedom?
NU3400		White Mountains
NU2927		Who Really Killed Cock Robin?
NU2080		Wind in the Willows
NU5969		Winter Room
NU6768	NU6776SP	Wringer
NU7284	NU7292SP	Year Down Yonder

Grades 7-8

NU4342		Acorn People
NU0916	NU4911SP	Across Five Aprils
NU3567	NU5284SP	Adventures of Tom Sawyer
NU6784	NU6792SP	All Alone in the Universe
NU6806	NU6814SP	And Then There Were None
NU0983	NU6078SP	Anne Frank: Diary of a Young Girl
NU3419		Anne of Green Gables
NU119X		April Morning
NU4814		Banner in the Sky
NU0924		Beat the Turtle Drum
NU0932		Big Red
NU1203		Big Wave
NU1483		Bless the Beasts and the Children
NU5826	NU5834SP	Bomb
NU6639		Brady
NU7322	NU7330SP	Brian's Winter
NU2455	NU492XSP	Call It Courage
NU1386	NU5292SP	Call of the Wild
NU4822		Canyons
NU3141	NU4121SP	Cay
NU1394		Cheaper by the Dozen
NU7384		Children of the River
NU6175		Christmas Carol
NU1211	NU6086SP	Contender
NU3931	NU394XSP	Day No Pigs Would Die
NU1408		Deathwatch
NU4385		Dicey's Song
NU3427		Dogsong
NU7349	NU7357SP	Dragon's Gate
NU0738		Dragonwings
NU0991		Farewell to Manzanar
NU4083	NU4091SP	Flowers for Algernon
NU900X	NU9018SP	Freak the Mighty
NU1513		Gentlehands
NU6183	NU7171SP	Giver
NU4228	NU8372SP	Great Gilly Hopkins
NU1238	NU4938SP	Hatchet
NU7996		Haymeadow
NU6121	NU613XSP	Heaven
NU2536	NU8283SP	Hobbit
NU6148	NU6156SP	Holes
NU1246		Homecoming
NU7381	NU739XSP	Hope Was Here
NU5160	NU8321SP	House of Dies Drear
NU580X	NU5818SP	I am the Cheese
NU1424		I Heard the Owl Call My Name
NU2293		I Know What You Did Last Summer
NU1254		Incident at Hawk's Hill
NU4687	NU4695SP	Incredible Journey
NU2021		Izzy, Willy-Nilly
NU1262	NU8364SP	Jacob Have I Loved
NU1270	NU5306SP	Johnny Tremain
NU4857		Journey
NU1025	NU8216SP	Julie of the Wolves
NU377X	NU3788SP	Just Dial a Number
NU1947	NU3435SP	Killing Mr. Griffin
NU1033		King of the Wind
NU1432		Language of the Goldfish
NU4660	NU4679SP	Light in the Forest

NU5179		Lincoln: A Photobiography
NU630X	NU6318SP	Little Women
NU6164	NU6172SP	Man Who Was Poe
NU8011	NU802XSP	Midwife's Apprentice
*NU7209	NU7217SP	Miracle's Boys
NU1831	NU5314SP	Miracle Worker
NU1041		Moves Make the Man
NU2730	NU5322SP	Mrs. Frisby and the Rats of NIMH
NU380X	NU8232SP	My Brother Sam is Dead
*NU7225	NU7233SP	My Louisiana Sky
NU1068	NU4946SP	My Side of the Mountain
NU7392		No Promises in the Wind
NU7406		Nothing But the Truth
NU5893	NU5907SP	Out of the Dust
NU3621	NU4067SP	Outsiders
NU3257	NU3265SP	Pearl
NU3893	NU3907SP	Pigman
NU198X		Pistachio Prescription
NU4407	NU4415SP	Red Pony
NU5977		Riddle of Penncroft Farm
NU5985		Rifles for Watie
NU6116		River
NU8186	NU8194SP	Samurai's Tale
NU4865		Sarah Bishop
NU2935		Scorpions
NU6326	NU6334SP	Shabanu: Daughter of the Wind
NU1084		Shadow of a Bull
•NU7462	NU7470SP	Shiva's Fire
NU2420	NU4954SP	Sign of the Beaver
NU1335		Slave Dancer
NU184X		Snow Bound
NU5788	NU5796SP	So Far from the Bamboo Grove
NU1459		Solitary Blue
NU1106	NU4962SP	Sounder
NU1114		Soup
*NU7268	NU7276SP	Space Station Seventh Grade
NU5702	NU5710SP	Staying Fat for Sarah Byrnes
NU5993		Stonewall
NU7414		Streams to the River, River to the Sea
NU1122		Summer of Fear
NU1130		Summer of My German Soldier
NU6687	NU6695SP	Tangerine
NU6709	NU6717SP	Tears of a Tiger
NU1955		Tiger Eyes
NU8844	NU8852SP	Tiger, Tiger, Burning Bright
NU7422		Timothy of the Cay
NU8860	NU8879SP	Toughing It
NU6000		Traitor: The Case of Benedict Arnold
NU6493		Transport 7-41-R
NU1343		Treasure Island
NU3761		Twenty-One Balloons
NU7708	NU7716SP	Walk Two Moons
NU8143	NU8151SP	Weirdo
NU7430	NU8038SP	West Against the Wind
NU4644	NU4652SP	Westing Game
NU4229	NU4237SP	When the Legend Die
NU6741	NU675XSP	When Zachary Beaver Came to Town
NU6342	NU6350SP	Where the Lilies Bloom
NU2447	NU4907SP	Where the Red Fern Grows
NU3362	NU5276SP	White Fang
NU2463	NU5349SP	Witch of Blackbird Pond
NU4172		Woodsong
NU1181	NU4989SP	Wrinkle in Time
NU8887	NU8895SP	Z for Zachariah
NU7047	NU7055SP	Zlata's Diary

Grades 9-12

NU1823	NU3087SP	Adventures of Huckleberry Finn
NU6191	NU6205SP	All Quiet on the Western Front
NU9131	NU914XSP	All the Pretty Horses
NU6180	NU6199SP	Animal Dreams
NU3052	NU3060SP	Animal Farm
NU7449	NU7457SP	Antigone
NU5532	NU5540SP	As I Lay Dying
NU5047	NU5055SP	As You Like It
NU8909	NU8917SP	Bean Trees
NU9158	NU9166SP	Billy Budd
NU6202	NU6210SP	Black Boy
NU8062	NU8070SP	Bless Me, Ultima
*NU708X	NU7098SP	Bluest Eye
NU4458	NU4466SP	Brave New World
NU5063	NU5071SP	Cannery Row
NU9190	NU9204SP	Canterbury Tales
NU4490	NU4504SP	Catcher in the Rye
NU2064	NU6299SP	Chocolate War
NU7465	NU7473SP	Chosen
NU508X	NU5098SP	Cold Sassy Tree
*NU7128	NU7136SP	Count of Monte Cristo
NU363X	NU3648SP	Crucible
NU3540	NU3559SP	Cry, the Beloved Country
NU6213	NU6221SP	Cyrano de Bergerac
NU7481	NU749XSP	Dandelion Wine
NU5101	NU511XSP	David Copperfield
NU1491		Death Be Not Proud
NU1858	NU3850SP	Death of a Salesman
NU8925	NU8933SP	Doll's House/ Hedda Gabler
NU6229	NU6237SP	Downriver
NU6504	NU6512SP	Dracula
NU1505		Effect of Gamma Rays on Man-in-the-Moon Marigolds
NU5128	NU5136SP	Ethan Frome
NU301X	NU3028SP	Fahrenheit 451
NU6369	NU6377SP	Fallen Angels
NU4547	NU4555SP	Farewell to Arms
NU7503	NU7511SP	Frankenstein
NU6865	NU6873SP	Gathering of Old Men
NU1866	NU3370SP	Glass Menagerie
NU6520	NU6539SP	Good Earth
NU2994	NU3001SP	Grapes of Wrath
NU5144	NU5152SP	Great Expectations
NU3168	NU3176SP	Great Gatsby
NU9212	NU9220SP	Gulliver's Travels
NU4180	NU4199SP	Hamlet
NU3729	NU3737SP	Heart is a Lonely Hunter
NU6245	NU6253SP	Hear of Darkness/ Secret Sharer
NU136X		Hiroshima
NU4830	NU5591SP	House on Mango Street
NU4849	NU6345SP	I Know Why the Caged Bird Sings
NU752X	NU7538SP	Iliad
NU658X	NU6598SP	Inferno
NU6601	NU661XSP	Inherit the Wind
NU5605	NU5613SP	Ironman
NU7546	NU7554SP	Ishi, Last of His Tribe
NU4628	NU4636SP	Jane Eyre
NU8941	NU895XSP	Joy Luck Club
NU3036	NU3044SP	Julius Caesar
NU9239	NU9247SP	King Lear
NU6628	NU6636SP	Last of the Mohicans
NU7562	NU7570SP	Les Miserables
•NU742X	NU7438SP	Lesson Before Dying
*NU7187	NU7195SP	Little Prince
NU5648	NU5656SP	Long Day's Journey Into Night
NU3834	NU3842SP	Lord of the Flies
NU4369	NU4377SP	Macbeth
NU5745	NU5753SP	Madame Bovary
NU3508	NU3516SP	Mayor of Casterbridge
NU5664	NU5672SP	Merchant of Venice
•NU7446	NU7454SP	Metamorphosis
NU5187	NU5195SP	Midsummer Night's Dream
NU6881	NU689XSP	Monster
NU9255	NU9263SP	Much Ado About Nothing

NU...29	NU7597SP	My Antonia
	NU8178SP	Mythology
	NU6248SP	Native Son
	NU8054SP	Night
	NU4148SP	1984
	NU7619SP	Odyssey
NU7627	NU7635SP	Oedipus the King
NU1874	NU3109SP	Of Mice and Men
NU4032	NU4040SP	Old Man and the Sea
NU5209	NU5217SP	Othello
NU6256	NU6264SP	Our Town
*NU7241	NU725XSP	Picture of Dorian Gray
NU7643	NU7651SP	Portrait of the Artist as a Young Man
NU766X	NU7678SP	Pride and Prejudice
NU9271	NU928XSP	Pygmalion
NU3125	NU3133SP	Raisin in the Sun
NU6660	NU6679SP	Rebecca
NU346X	NU3478SP	Red Badge of Courage
NU3745	NU3753SP	Romeo and Juliet
NU1440		Rumble Fish
NU3389	NU3397SP	Scarlet Letter
NU6385	NU6393SP	Scarlet Pimpernel
NU8968	NU8976SP	Sense and Sensibility
NU3990	NU4008SP	Separate Peace
NU2773	NU5330SP	Shane
NU6946	NU6954SP	Siddhartha
NU6407	NU6415SP	Slam!
•NU7500	NU7519SP	Slaughterhouse-Five
NU5842	NU5850SP	Snow Falling on Cedars
NU8828	NU8836SP	Song of Be
NU9379	NU9387SP	Song of Solomon
NU6989	NU6997SP	Speak
NU9298	NU9301SP	Stranger
NU4326	NU4334SP	Tale of Two Cities
NU7686	NU7694SP	Taming of the Shrew
NU6272	NU6280SP	Tempest
NU4261	NU427XSP	Tess of the D'Urbervilles
NU1467		Tex
NU5225	NU5233SP	That Was Then, This Is Now
NU8089	NU8097SP	Their Eyes Were Watching God
NU8127	NU8135SP	Things Fall Apart
NU7004	NU7012SP	Three Musketeers
NU1572	NU3079SP	To Kill a Mockingbird
NU931X	NU9328SP	Turn of the Screw
NU5869	NU5877SP	Twelfth Night
NU7020	NU7039SP	War of the Worlds
NU6423	NU6431SP	Watership Down
NU6725	NU6733SP	Wave
NU4598	NU4601SP	Wuthering Heights
NU9336	NU9344SP	Yellow Raft in Blue Water

Additional Products

NU783XRH	Graphic Organizer Collection
NU5885RH	Holocaust: Study Guide
NU5966RH	Novel News
NU8437RH	Reacting To Literature: Writing Activities for Every Book Gr. 6-8
NU5524RH	Reacting To Literature: Writing Activities for Every Book Gr. 9-12
NU5958RH	Tackling Literary Terms
NU9395RH	Teaching Viewing
NU8453RH	Writing Projects for Literature

Please contact us if you do not see the title you are looking for. We are always adding new titles.

SP indicates Student Packet for this title.   * Fall 2001 title   • Spring 2002 title

Novel Units® Teacher Guides and Student Packets— created by teachers for teachers!

Easy-to-use with all the tools you need to teach a novel!

We have Teacher Guides for all the books you want to teach and your students want to read.

Each Teacher Guide includes:

- a story summary
- prereading activities
- vocabulary exercises
- comprehension strategies
- discussion questions
- critical thinking challenges
- literary analysis questions and activities
- assessment tools
- graphic organizers
- writing ideas
- art ideas
- and more!

Also Available:
Student Packets

With fully reproducible pages, each Student Packet includes:

- study questions
- vocabulary activities
- comprehension activities
- project and essay ideas
- comprehension quizzes
- unit test

ISBN 1-56137-247-1

Self Scoring
Adult Personality Assessment Profile

What Makes You Tick

Identifying Your Strengths, Struggles and Emotional Needs

Kathryn Robbins and Cassandra Cooper